Bradley Tice

A Universal Archetype Computer System

GRIN Publishing

Imprint:

Copyright © 2012 GRIN Verlag GmbH
Print and binding: Books on Demand GmbH, Norderstedt Germany
ISBN: 978-3-656-64528-3

A Universal Archetype Computer System

By Dr. Bradley S. Tice, Advanced Human Design P.O. Turlock, California 95380 U.S.A.

Abstract

The paper will examine the nature and development of a proto-type computer system that is based on the fundamentals of a successive addition of like-natured characters found in a binary sequential string. Arabic numerals will represent each character type and will be summed as input into the computer and compressed into like-natured sub-groups for storage and future de-compression as output. Both the random and non-random binary sequential strings are compressed by this system and are a functional model for both a finite state and infinite state machines.

Introduction

This computer system was designed by the author from fundamental work in the area of algorithmic complexity [1] & [2]. The system uses the input of a traditional binary sequential string of Arabic numerals that is read and compressed into sub-groups of like-natured characters, such as 1's with other 1's and 0's with other 0's, and single character types and maintains the exact character type and location from the original input binary sequential string. The stored data can be de-compressed to the exact model of the original input string for output.

An example for a non-random series of a sequential binary string for input is as follows:

Example #1
[10101010101010101010]

With a series of 1's and 0's making a total of 20 characters in a regular pattern of sequences that can be stored as [10] multiplied by ten as there are ten 1's and ten 0's with

the 0's following the 1's in an alternating fashion with the 1's the initial position in a series of ten sets of [10].

The resulting compression can be recorded as [10] x 10 which saves on space for transmission and storage of the information.

The example for a random series of a sequential binary string for input is a follows:

Example #2
[00011000010111000111]

With a series of sub-groups of 0's and 1's that can be compressed into each sub-group of a common like-natured character, either a 0 or a 1 in the initial position for each sub-group. Example #2 separated into each sub-group would appear as follows:

[000]+[11]+[0000]+[1]+[0]+[111]+[000]+[111]

The separated character sub-groups can be compressed by using each sub-group's initial character and a symbol for the multiplication of that character and the number of multiples that character contains such as the character 1 is repeated three times in the last sub-group in Example #2 that is [111] and can be compressed as [1]x3 or simplified by using a notation system to represent the multiple of three such as underlining the character 1, [1], to the character to represent]1]x3.

Being specific with the underlined character 1 to represent a multiple of three 1's, [111], in the Example #2 of the random sequential binary string, the following specific compressions will occur:

Example #2 Specific Compression:
[000]+[11]+[0000]+[1]+[0]+[1]+[000]+[1]

The original 20 character length is reduced to a 16 character length in a specifically compressed state. This means less space taken up for storage to represent the same amount as the original 20 character random sequential binary string. Decompression reproduces the original character number and type on the random sequential binary string for transmission or output.

A whole or 'universal' compression of Example #2 random sequential binary string would allow for all sub-groups of the string to be compressed into a sequential binary string that is less than the original 'non-compressed' state while allowing for a complete de-compression of the string to the original length and form of the pre-input random sequential binary string. These properties are also true for the non-random sequential binary string.

Note: Remember that each character in a sequential line is the Arabic symbol and not the numeric value of that character. In other words the character 1 is the opposite of the character 0 only and quantitatively not the value of 1, one, verses 0, zero, values. The characters used for the examples could have been from the English alphabet rather than the Arabic numerical system with A being used for 0 and B being used for 1. This qualitative and quantitative partitioning of symbols is by way of Shannon [3].

Foundations

The foundations for this computer system come from Post (1936) and Kleene (1952) as discussed by Minsky (1967) [4], [5] & [6]. The 'summing engine' aspect to the computer system is by way of the author's fundamental work in the area of algorithmic complexity starting in 1998 with the finding of an algorithmic program that was able to compress a random binary sequential string [7]. The minimal weight of the semantic aspects to the character types is from Shannon [8].

Finite State Machine

All finite state machines are time sensitive and discrete in manner and follow a sequence of actions and be predisposed to determinism [9]. The author's computer system has the following components that satisfy the above mentioned criteria for a finite state machine: an Input, a

Reader/Scanner, Storage and an Output.

Infinite State Machine

The same components are found in the infinite state machine; Input, Reader/Scanner, Storage and Output, but the nature of the process is infinite. To side step the need for an infinite storage system, a closed infinite loop for input can be used that would stop storing data once a completed cycle had finished, a finite timeline, and allows the computer system to continue operations ad infinitum [10]. The magnitude for an indefinitely large finite set can be at a level that approaches an infinity without becoming an unworkable absurd abstract [11]. Also computing components can be replaced over time to make it a continuous process to be extended indefinitely over time [12].

List of Instructions

Minsky has noted that Wang (1957) has the shortest list of instructions known for a computer at four sequential instructions [13]. The author's computer system has two:

Read/Scan with the act of storage of information being implied in the command.

De-compression and output of all input sequential string information that was stored.

Universal Qualities

While this paper has focused on binary sequential strings only, the author has expanded beyond the traditional radix 2, or binary, level to include all known radix based numbers and has examined and tested the radix 8. radix 10, radix 12 and radix 16 based number systems while using the algorithmic complexity system used for this computer system [14].

Summary

This summing engine type of computer system is capable of compressing both random and non-random binary sequential strings of input and storing the saved data for output. The computer system also has the shortest list of instructions known.

References

[1] B.S. Tice, "An Abstract on the Theory and Application of a Universal Archetype Computer", Unpublished Manuscript. Copyright 2012.

[2] B. Tice, "Aspects of Kolmogorov Complexity: The Physics of Information", Rivers Publishers, Denmark, 2009.

[3] Shannon, C.E. and W. Weaver, "The Mathematical Theory of Communication". The University of Illinois, Champaign-Urbana, 1949.

[4] M. Davis, "The Undecidable: Basic Papers on Undecidable Propositions, Unsolvable Problems and Computable Functions", Raven Press, Hewlett, New York. 1965, p. 289.

[5] S. C. Kleene, "Introduction to Metamathematics", Van Nostrand, New York, 1952, pp. 356-361.

[6] M. Minsky, "Computation: Finite and Infinite Machines", Prentice-Hall, Englewood Cliffs, New Jersey, 1967, pp. 262-265.

[7] Abide, Tice, 2009, pp. 47-52.

[8] C. Shannon and W. Weaver, "The Mathematical Theory of Communication", The University of Illinois, Champagne-Urbana, 1949.

[9] P.J. Denning, J.B. Dennis and J.E. Qualitz, "Machines, Languages and Computation", Prentice-Hall, Englewood Cliffs, New Jersey, 1978, pp. 88-89.

[10] M. Minsky, "Computation: Finite and infinite Machines", Prentice-Hall, Englewood cliffs, New Jersey, 1967, p. 115.

[11] B.S. Tice, "The Limits of Infinity", Paper presented at the 78th Annual Meeting of the Pacific Division of the AAAS, June 22-26, 1997, Corvallis, Oregon.

[12] J. Von Neumann, "Theory of Self-Reproducing Automata", University of Illinois, Urbana, Edited by A.W. Burks, 1966, p. 20.

[13] Abide, Minsky, 1967, pp. 262-265.

[14] B.S. Tice, "A Level of Martin-Lof Randomness", Science Publishers, New Hampshire, 2012.